# RESILIENCE

## Mervin Scott

ISBN: 978-1-916981-71-3
Paperback edition

All poems by Mervin Scott

Cover illustrations by Aurelie Freoua

Editing by Andy Finney

You may email the author at
mervinscott@pnauthor.com

# CONTENTS

# HYPOCRISY AND SOCIETY

# DISPENSABLE NUMBERS

Each day runs by,
pray to the sky.
Labouring for peanuts
leaves me broke,
I don't know how long patience will cope.
Lack of care is the subject,
I am just a dispensable object.
Management who programme staff
to do incredible tasks,
looking up to see people looking down,
finding it amusing
in thinking that they are better;
or I can always be unemployed,
where names truly have no sound.
Compelled to receive this,
a kind of blackmail.

# GOD OF MONEY

Enslaved by necessity, these paper chains
are so hard to break;
sacrificing a life to work,
worshipping money seven days a week,
what is given is taken back by
never-ending bills,
yet praying for deliverance from my debts,
seeking your comforts and benefits.
Your promises may be hollow,
but I work towards a better tomorrow.
When will it come?
Thy will be done on Earth, to create
a man-made Heaven.
So, give me today my daily bread,
forgive me when I trespass against you.
For mine will be
the power and the glory,
(But not) forever and ever.

Amen.

# PAPER GUN

Buy the newspaper.
Believe it harmless as a paper gun.
Advertisements everywhere,
persuasion with all sorts of gimmicks.
Buy a newspaper to feed your brain,
putting to rest your inquisitive mind.
Whilst you read, we cook up more
black and white pulp to be
consistently devoured.
Deceit is the main ingredient.
A paper without scandal is like
a gun without bullets.
The truth does not sell.
Our paper is not plain, it is loaded.
So put it to your head and
pull the trigger daily.

# THE CITY

The city is like a fast woman.
The businessmen are
her pimps.
I don't trust her, so I kiss
with my eyes open.
The truth is disguised by an expensive
scent to absorb the stench.
She is dishonourable, yet the blind
clothe her with respect.
She is very attractive and costly to befriend.
She will entertain you
with short-lived happiness,
until your money is spent.
Now you have no friends.

# THE PIGEONS

I am a pigeon, waiting for the fat
to finish their meal, so they can
throw their crumbs to the floor for me to eat.
Before the feed even touches the ground,
other pigeons come from nowhere,
their beaks numb to the flavours
of contentment.
No time for friendship,
the grasping of bread from
each other's beaks.
Who cares, lies, cheats, steals, kills?
Every pigeon for itself.
Just because you can fly,
it does not mean you are free.

# LITTLE

Awake from my little bed,
in my little room,
in my little flat,
have a wash
in my little bathroom,
put on my suit and
tie my tie into a little knot.
I'm on my way to my little job
and my little desk
overflowing with work
and no window.
The big company
with workers and their little dreams,
who talk about the weather
and live for the weekend.
And at the end of my long hours,
at my little desk overflowing
with work and no window,
I join the flock of commuters
at the station
and enter the big train with little room
for more of the same tomorrow.

# THE WEATHER IS TWO-FACED

I drew back my curtains
to witness a pleasant morning.
The weather appeared to be
nice and bright,
fooling me to lower my guard.
I dressed light and
forgot that a bright day
could still be freezing.
At my most vulnerable,
it started raining.
The next day, I woke up
to see another pleasant morning.
It did not fool me.

# LAND OF VULNERABLE EMOTIONS

# BRIEF ENCOUNTER

In your expression I searched for sentiment,
yet all I found was ignorance.
We were so distant that day,
like a kiss separated from touch
by a cold pane of glass.
It was a brief encounter
lasting for what seemed like ages,
until you walked into the past.
Regret cuts me like pieces of glass,
only silence was spoken.
I don't know when but I know
I'm going to see you again someday,
even if it's only by coincidence.

# DEFINITELY MISSING YOU

I'm definitely missing you and if
you're definitely missing me too,
just look up.
Even if the sky is grey,
beyond the dark clouds there is sunshine
to remind us of the happy times we shared.
Although you're far away,
these warm thoughts keep me so close
that I can hear your heart beat.
I don't know what it is that I miss
about you the most,
but it's definitely your silky hair,
definitely your nice eyes,
definitely your smile so bright,
definitely your gentle voice,
definitely your loving arms.
Kind, soft hands and tender touch.
But most important of all is your
sincere heart which does not wrinkle or scar,
for your true beauty lies within.

# DINNER FOR TWO

She sounded surprised and said
she was flattered that I remembered,
but how could I forget the first time we met?
Her sweet voice awakens the feelings
I once felt.
I wanted to see her again,
to express the way I honestly felt,
so I prepared a surprise meal for two,
but I didn't give her time to chew.
I misunderstood everything and gave
her too much too soon;
she brought it all back up.
I forgot to season the food
with Patience.
Have I scared her away
through my lack of judgment?
Everything I wanted to say over
a period of many years, I said
in a few minutes.

# DOUBTS

Is my love a love
you can be sure of?
Sometimes the clouds
cast over the night sky,
but it does not mean that
the moon and stars are not there.
Clouds of doubt
hide the night sky,
but in the morning we never doubt,
with daylight showing us the way.
If it rains it will soon become dry,
if it is cold we can go somewhere warm.

# GREEN, GREEN GRASS

Is there a time and a place
in your past,
where your memory fears to tread?
When you're there you despair,
you feel so cold, so strange;
you have tried to forgive but
your clenched fist refuses to let go.
This place in your past did not
begin as a frozen wilderness;
it was once green and lush,
but time has frozen still,
at that day, at that year
that changed your life.
The only way to melt the ice
is to forgive and forget,
day by day, year by year,
until you can once again see
nothing but green, green grass.

# THE HAVE AND THE HAVE NOT GOT

Missing someone I have not got
that I never had
and probably never will have.
The chances that I had
I have not got.
Thinking of what I could've had
can drive me mad,
for what I have not got
someone else has.

# SPRING

# WARRIOR KING

I am the mighty axe in the hands of the Warrior King,
the LORD God Almighty.
Every adversary will be struck down to make way for the
Prince of Peace.
At the sight of his axe, terror will strike the camp of the
wicked,
for it is time for the forest of Evil to be cut down and thrown
into the fire.
I have been unleashed,
I will not be withdrawn,
until every form of Evil that has tried to raise its ugly head
above the name of the LORD had been destroyed;
for I am the warrior who knows the God he serves.
I will attain the unattainable.
The light has come to displace the darkness.
I am the roaring fire,
where warring angels make their camp.
As I open my mouth,
the enemy will run for cover and find no place to hide,
other than the lake of burning fire.
Even fear will be fearful of the words
that come from my mouth.
Death will try to hold me and fail.
The dragon will swallow me, thinking that I am no more,
but I will cut through the back of his neck
with the Sword of the Living God.
Every hope of the enemy will be slain.
To all nobles of darkness,

from the highest to the lowest,
this is the day of the LORD God Almighty.
Such confusion will befall your Kingdom,
that demon will attack demon.
They will not know their left from their right,
their legs will tremble;
for the Sword of Judgement is coming!
Your armies will drown in the innocent blood of the Lamb.
Every messenger will fill your ears with bad report.
Every throne of darkness will be engulfed with
the terror of the true God.
This is the vengeance.
A day of victory,
a day of thanksgiving to all those who are righteous,
a day of dread to all those who bow down
to false gods and wickedness.

# THE WAR CHORUS

Arise you mighty warriors, you chosen few,
commissioned by the God of War.
Shake off the self-pity,
stand firm, you are on solid ground.
Adorn the full armour of God,
open your doubtful eyes and have faith in the shield
that protects your precious life.
Do not be intimidated by your enemies who
outnumber and surround you.
This is a great day for miracles and blessings.
Look up towards the God of triumph;
you are in the presence of victory.
Be joyful and sing praises unto the LORD your God,
and the kingdom of darkness will be filled with terror.
Who is Death that we should fear him?
The kingdom of Heaven is a breath away!
Fire of God, come down and consume
this pungent smell of pride and arrogance.
Pour confusion on the counsel of the wicked,
the conquering lion has risen.
It is time to fight the Fight of Faith.
Warring angels, go forth, the banner of Judah
will not fall to the ground,
our battle cry alone will bring down the walls of timidness.
Archers, dip your arrows in the fire of God,
keen eyes and a steadfast hand never miss the target.
My sword is thirsty and
my horse is prepared for battle;

my eyes will not retreat and my heart will not surrender.
A bitter defeat awaits the enemy,
and the treasures of darkness
will be an offering unto the Living God.

# NO SURRENDER

Poverty has laid siege, in hope that
I surrender the splendour with which
the LORD has blessed me.
Madness tries to break down the walls of sanity,
pride rots away the city gate,
moths gorge the garments of praise,
locusts have eaten the harvest,
disease has contaminated the water well,
sickness has destroyed my cattle.
I can hear the footsteps of famine
marching towards my kingdom.
Hostile arrows fall from the sky,
the ruler of darkness desires to
steal my crown,
he wants to chain me to my inequities
like a slave.
His term of surrender is death.
The Shield of Faith grows heavier
with every step.
Fist to fist, sword to sword.
I have slain many, but the enemy keeps on attacking.
It seems the war will never end.
For how long will I cry out in distress?
Am I not a Son of Righteousness?
Through God's grace it was then that I remembered
the revelation of eternal hope
where there are no shadows of doubt.
Cursed are those who rise up

against the LORD's anointed.
The God of Israel will subdue
the mighty waves of oppression.
The flood of tyranny will never go beyond
the white cliffs of salvation.
Tired and wounded soldier, the arrows
of fear, confusion, frustration and sickness are many,
but the righteous shall prevail.
Be bold. Be strong.
Pull the arrows of depression from your flesh.
Do not allow the double-edged sword
to fall from your hand.
In the heat of battle, death is never satisfied.
Was it not the LORD God Almighty,
the Chief Strategist who parted the Red Sea,
allowing Israel to cross on dry ground,
closing the sea, causing Egypt's armies to drown?
Was it not the same God who gave us this land,
flowing with milk and honey?
This is my inheritance, not my grave.
The LORD did not bring us
this far to be slain.
Today is a day of praise,
a day when every enemy surrenders.
A day when every knee bends and
every head bows to the name of the LORD.
Let there be light,
let there be life.
Let there be victory for the chosen generation of
no compromise, no surrender.

# SPIRITUAL BOLDNESS

My enemies have thrown me to the ground
in hope that I might be shattered,
but there is a righteous God
who sits on the throne of Heaven.
If it was not for the LORD on that day,
Death would have overcome me.
The LORD has revived my soul with a new wine;
words of faith flow from my mouth.
The Word of God is the
cushion where I lay my head.
The LORD will give me rest from my adversaries.
In the midst of chaos I will be at peace,
for my confidence is in the LORD
and not my own strength.
The hands of fear will squeeze,
but I will not become dry,
for I have become saturated in
Spiritual Boldness.
The enemies who held me captive
will be conquered.
Victory upon victory awaits all those who have
the faith and courage to confront their fears.

# JUDAS

Your rags have been cleansed by
the blood of the Lamb,
yet you continue to wear
pure white robes on filthy skin,
all your shouting, praising and
singing for everyone to see.
You have betrayed the LORD with a kiss,
you deceive yourself by living a lie.
Everything you do behind closed doors
will be made public.
You're like a cockroach who runs
for darkness after
light has entered the room.
The Father of Lies will not be
there to shelter you from the truth.
Struggle and fight with all your might;
the layers of lies will be removed,
exposing your true likeness.

# FATTENED CALF

You took me into your care,
making me feel like a pampered pet,
showering me with hollow compliments.
Like an innocent lamb, I was being
fattened with lies to be sacrificed.
You sat me in a comfortable cauldron
whilst all along I was being cooked;
staring at the lid of fear
whilst being drained of life.
Nothing burns more than
the flames of betrayal,
for you can only see the light of truth
when the heat is on.

# ZIKLAG

Ziklag is a place where everything you hold dear is destroyed,
your hopes for tomorrow in ashes.
A place where your valuables are carried off.
A place where your sons and daughters are taken captive.
A place of intense distress.
A place where you are stripped of every confidence.
A place where your family will talk against you,
friends will talk of stoning you within a second,
betraying the love that was shared
over many years.
Ziklag is a place of tears.
Though my heart is heavy,
the LORD will lighten my load.
My strength, my hope is truly in the LORD,
for He came down from His throne
to live amongst men,
because He saw me and He knew me.
He went through 40 bitter days and
40 bitter nights in the desert to be tempted,
because He saw me and He knew me.
He went through betrayal and insults,
because He saw me and He knew me.
He died, and on the third day He rose again,
because He saw me and He knew me.
That is why my confidence is in the LORD,
for He saw my trial and torture
whilst He was on the cross,
and is with me throughout.

Every plan to destroy me will be frustrated
and confused.
Every enemy who rises against me
will be put to shame,
for the LORD will pursue my enemies
and overcome them.
The LORD will surely return everything
that was stolen,
for Ziklag is a place where God
performs miracles.

# SUMMER

# ACT I

**The Messenger:**
    Should I hate God?
    Did the Lord Jesus get flogged by scorpions?
    Tied with barbed wire to an iron cross,
    dreams infiltrated by nightmares of
    friends betraying you;
    family hating you,
    being torn to pieces by machine devices?
    Nothing that I have committed
    is worth this curse.
    I'm reaping the Hell I did not sow;
    I'm sure even Satan is confused.
    Accessed by a young doctor,
    a most perfect woman in a mad house,
    at my most broken and vulnerable.
    This is the evil timing of Man.
    Why couldn't we be like Adam and Eve,
    Romeo and Juliet with no tragedy?
    Why couldn't we have met
    for the first time through kind introduction?
    Making notes of my answers to her questions,
    holding the pen with her
    beautiful slim fingers.
    It seems the wisdom of King Solomon
    has been hidden in a woman
    who I'm sure is the original beautiful
    Queen of the South reincarnated
    as a female King Solomon.

Impressive mathematics.
I'll seduce her with a Cartier pen
and a note saying,
"I thought of you all summer,
wishing tomorrow was Christmas."


**The Warlock King:**

Where does the dark-skinned Lord
eat his meat and drink his water?


**The 1st Duke:**

In our most confused he is there,
in the heat of our battle,
holding the line.
He disappears before we can
give cheer and our thanks
for his courage.
It has been noted that your
eldest daughter is secretly
joining the order of nuns.


**The Warlock King:**

My two daughters,
the dark-skinned Lord has met the meat of
my eldest daughter.
Her younger sister will kill him
when he next drinks water.

Spy on my eldest daughter;
if she hides her wisdom in
her excrement, I want you to
eat it and tell me what
goes on in her conniving head.


END OF ACT I

# ACT II

**Eldest Child and**
**Daughter of the**
**Warlock King:**

> You're late my Lord!
> I have been studying your God
> and I am sure you are Jacob.
> Toiling this land for my father's
> two daughters.
> All these years you have been going
> to the house of your LORD, tending the
> Reverend's land and at the end of God's labour,
> his daughters say they only want union with doctors and
> lawyers.
> Come, come, my Lord are you sure
> you have not yet been to the madhouse?

**The Messenger:**

> Your devil-worshipping younger brothers,
> who lost their virginity shagging
> dead women, trade no more
> insults, my dear.

**Eldest Daughter:**

> King David, who took five smooth
> stones from the brook to slay Goliath.
> Of your five brothers, how many
> have not yet gone to prison?
> You could only have one stone left,
> shepherd boy.
> Aim very carefully.

**The Messenger:**

> It seems you know the Word
> of God very well, my Lady.
> You will make an excellent Queen,
> for nothing seems to escape you.
> Does your father, the King, know
> that his life is under threat?
> What happened to us?

**Eldest Daughter:**

> I have a younger sister,
> that is what happened.
> I'm sure you know that she is
> no longer the little girl you knew
> in the playground.
> You said I was your Blondie 1979.

**The Messenger:**

It is time to make haste, my Lady.


**Eldest Daughter:**

Make haste, my Lord and messenger,
to see my younger sister?
How did you keep warm these harsh winter months?
Did you drink vodka from her womb? If high winds
blast you off your motorbike, it is only my temper.


END OF ACT II

# ACT III

**The Messenger:**
> I envy this poem that I am writing to you.
> With a loving kiss, my message is
> without my lips, but I can imagine
> how your lips may taste.
> It has no eyes with which to recognise your face,
> no nose to smell your scent,
> no hands to touch your smooth, soft skin.
> It is only a poem and can not attain all this.
> Yet I envy this poem, inches from
> your lips, held in your hands,
> being looked upon by your bright eyes.
> Put my poem against your heart,
> just say you love the feeling,
> so that I can touch you with words.
> Can you imagine?

**Youngest Child and**
**Daughter of the**
**Warlock King:**
> I envy this poem,
> this is a nice verse.
> Make guitar strings from my hair
> and put these words to song.
> We'll make a bounty
> so you never have to ride that
> motorbike again.

How many times have you fallen off
that metal horse?


**The Messenger:**
How many times have you had lovers
in the night?


**Youngest Daughter:**
That many times it must have hurt.
If you read in the press that I am
in love with a fool
pay them no mind.
What will the papers say of me and you?


**The Messenger:**
The junkie and the madman
the new King and Queen of Bohemia.
They will put the paper gun to both
of us and blow our heads off
with insults.


**Youngest Daughter:**
Shall I commit suicide?

# AUTUMN

# PRICELESS LOVE

O LORD my God, even the great sea
hears Your voice,
for You command the tides to retreat and rise,
You summon awesome winds and the trees
lose their leaves in respect to the season.
The birds know where to migrate,
the animals know where to hibernate:
You orchestrate nature with a word,
the Earth rotates and the Sun will
illuminate the Moon to distinguish
night from day.
It reveals the great constellations magnifying
Your glory giving greater navigation to life.
Yet, LORD, Your most beautiful creation is
the daughter who is
righteous in Your sight.
She is priceless, more scarce than gold.
Although I walk through the Garden of Eden,
my heart is in the wilderness,
for I am lonely without her love.
Lay me down to sleep, O LORD,
and take a rib from the cage that protects
my heart from the forbidden fruits.
She will become bone of my bone,
flesh of my flesh, and together
we will forever be righteous in Your sight.

# EDEN

I have been wandering through this wilderness,
plagued with loneliness for so long,
that I count my shadow as a companion.
Although I can see it, I can never hold it.
I can give chase, yet never catch it.
My shadow is nowhere to be seen
when I'm alone in the cold darkness,
for my companion is only faithful
when I stand in the light.
I have been patient with this barren land
in the hope of finding the Garden of Life,
a garden where there are no tears of sorrow,
a garden where the fruits of love
grow freely,
a garden where the trees never lose their leaves
because it's always summer,
there is no darkness, just daylight.

# BUILDING THE BRIDGE OF LOVE

No bridge seems able to cross the
sea of insecurity between our worlds.
How can two people be so close
yet so far apart?
We have concealed
our love for so long
that it has become like holding one's breath.
I am sure neither of us can do this
for much longer,
my lungs are bursting to inhale
the fresh air of freedom.
We have to forget where we came from
and look ahead to where we're going.
Let us build a bridge of love.
We can cross the barriers of our
different worlds;
for the bricks will be made of
Patience and Hope,
the steel will be forged in
flames of Courage,
tempered in the sea of Security,
cemented by Trust,
too strong for anyone to tear down.
Only we can destroy what we have made.
I pray that day will never happen.

# WINTER

**Number 1 Boss:**

It has come to my attention
that our messenger has gone feral,
astray with a large deposit.
A deposit deemed forfeit
for not honouring an agreement.
Don't be fooled by this letterhead
from his lawyer.
It's in type but it's his handwriting.
Don't think for one minute
that all dark-skinned men are fools!
Yes, they kill the Daniel in their
generation with a life of crime,
but not this one; it has come
to my attention that he is a leader
in a Church.
It would have been better if he
got four female staff pregnant
and urinated on our floor,
than to walk off with our money.

**Number 3 Boss:**

Only four women pregnant, sir!

**Number 2 Boss:**

The man that leads the Church
is a good man, and they are good people.

44

**Number 3 Boss:**

He's not into man-to-man marking?
Is that the answer to the question
I did not ask?
You have been observing him, Number 2?


**Number 1 Boss:**

This time pay Judas 70 pieces of silver
instead of 30 so that he does not hang himself.
Every Sister within that Church that
he has spent more than two hours with
over the past ten years, watch over them
just in case she turns out to be Joan of Arc.
Turn his friends and any jilted lovers
against him. Send them corruption!
Send them war; if you turn him into a hero,
I will kill you both.
Be gone!

# RESILIENCE

Fortitude, resilience to overthinking, the walls which go beyond my limits, to imagine things that are not.

Tomorrow is a new day transcending doubts, pushing forwards, though the body says "rest" and suggests complacency, the enemy to new horizons.

I am the reason I have failed.

I am the reason I have succeeded.

With a simple choice to give in or go beyond.

Failures are there to remind us that tomorrow is another chance to try something different and evaluate your attempts to succeed.

You can't say no to the eagle when it wants to fly.

The capacity to recover quickly means a child will not always crawl because they fall over many times.

The destiny of a man is in how he will handle a challenge; experience is a good advisor.

I can attempt to climb a mountain but there is a right time of year, a right path and the right team of people, who can altogether equate to success at climbing the peak; this is experience.

A valuable friend to youth.

Go beyond your limits whilst you can imagine there is no end to a forest, whilst you can imagine no end to an ocean, no end to the sky.

Find the people who will find you, who share your passion.

The depth of your resilience is a silent agreement between madness and sanity.

May the walls never be breached by our imagination, staying safe with what is well known.

Fear is such a powerful weapon if you allow it to grow.

The need to feel accepted is a pitfall to truthful reasoning filled with compromise.

When pain comes to an end, suffering has its loss, memories of good times have their own way of healing.

Preparation defeats many a foe, but information is only useful to those who understand the logistics of when and how.